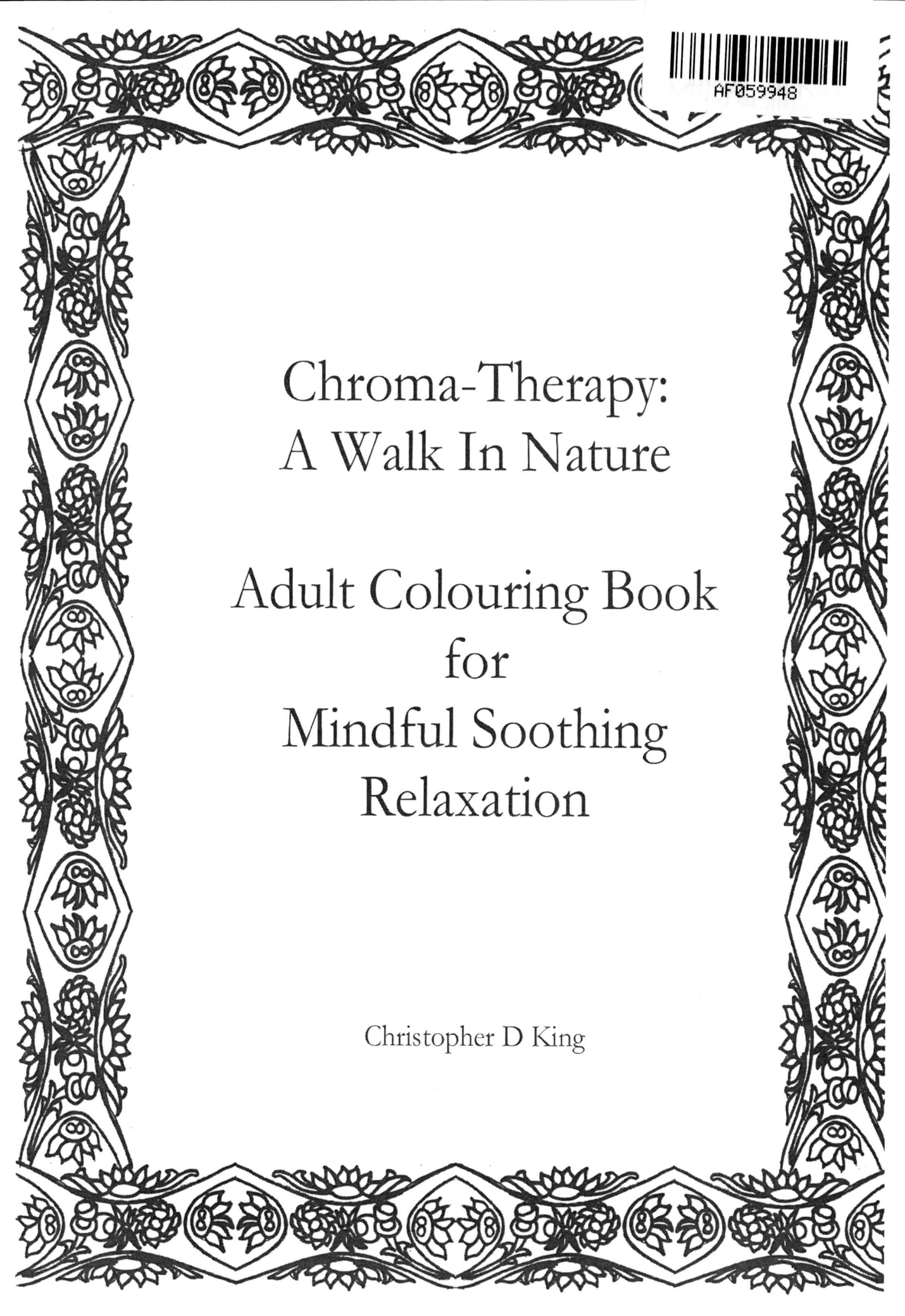

Chroma-Therapy: A Walk In Nature

Adult Colouring Book for Mindful Soothing Relaxation

Christopher D King

All images, illustrations and words contained in this
book are owned and are sole work and copyright
of the author/creator: Mr Christopher D King and
may not be copied, reproduced or recreated
wholly or partially without permission from the owner.

Copyright © Christopher D King (2016)

The right of Christopher D King to be identified as author of this
work has been asserted by him in accordance
with section 77 and 78 of the Copyright, Designs and Patents Act
1988.

All rights reserved. No part of this publication may be reproduced,
stored in a retrieval system,
or transmitted in any form or by any means, electronic, mechanical,
photocopying, recording, or
otherwise, without the prior permission of the publishers.
Any person who commits any unauthorized act in relation to this
publication may be liable to
criminal prosecution and civil claims for damages.

A CIP catalogue record for this title is available from the
British Library.

ISBN 9781787100770

www.austinmacauley.com
First Published (2016)
Austin Macauley Publishers Ltd.
25 Canada Square
Canary Wharf
London
E14 5LQ

DEDICATION

I'D LIKE TO DEDICATE MY FIRST PUBLISHED BOOK TO MY FIANCÉ, BUT MOST OF ALL TO HER PATIENCE! PERSEVERING LONG EVENINGS WITH THE SOUND OF MY PEN AND PENCIL SCRATCHING AWAY AT ANOTHER FRESH PAGE CAN'T HAVE BEEN EASY, BUT I COULDN'T HAVE DONE THIS WITHOUT YOUR SUPPORT, CHEER-LEADING AND OH YES – THOSE MAGNIFICENT FINE LINERS YOU GAVE ME!!

THE REASON I DRAW AND I DO THIS IS TO HELP KEEP MYSELF BALANCED. I KNOW THERE ARE LOTS OF PEOPLE OUT THERE – MY SISTER INCLUDED - WHO NEED TO KEEP THEIR MINDS OCCUPIED, OR JUST NEED SOME HELP SWITCHING INTO A MORE RELAXED MODE. I MIGHT NOT ALWAYS BE THERE FOR YOU, BUT THIS BOOK IS FOR YOU AND PEOPLE LIKE YOU WHOSE MIND JUST NEEDS HELP GETTING SOME PEACE EVERY NOW AND AGAIN.

WHENEVER I FEEL LIKE I NEED TO TUNE-OUT OR FOCUS ON SOMETHING I GO TO MY PENCIL AND PAD AND JUST START DRAWING. IT USUALLY STARTS WITH AN IDEA OR A CONCEPT, BUT IS ULTIMATELY JUST A VERY NICE WAY TO UNWIND AND DE-STRESS. I HOPE THAT YOU HAVE AS MUCH FUN AND HOURS OF ENGAGEMENT, AS I HAVE CREATING THESE ILLUSTRATIONS. BY HELPING ME TO FINISH THESE CREATIONS YOU'LL BE DOING ME A BIG FAVOUR – AS I REALLY DON'T WANT TO GO BACK AND HAVE TO COLOUR EVERYTHING IN MYSELF!!

I WOULD LOVE TO HEAR FROM YOU, SO PLEASE SEND COPIES OF YOUR COMPLETED DESIGNS TO MY EMAIL ADDRESS BELOW AND I'D LOVE TO POST SOME OF THE BEST INTERPRETATIONS ON MY WEBSITE. SOME OF THE PAGES ARE DELIBERATELY LEFT BLANK FOR YOU TO ADD YOUR OWN DESIGNS AND CREATIVITY TO. PLEASE WRITE TO:

cdkingbooks@gmail.com.

THANKS SO MUCH,

CHRIS.
@cdkingbooks
www.cdkingbooks.com

CONTENTS

ACKNOWLEDGEMENTS
TREE OF LIFE 1-4
CHAMELEON
ORNAMENTAL AQUARIUMS 1-4
DANDELION FOREST X 2
CROC-DETAIL & CROC
DRAGONFISH & PUFFER-FISH
GLASS-DRAGONFLY & BUGGIES
DOUBLE EAGLE
WISHING POND X 2
SECRET ANIMAL 2
FOX PLANTS & FOX-PRINCE
KISSING FROGS 1 and 2
GRASS-PLANTS & KING OF THE JUNGLE
LIZARD FOREST X 2
LEOPARD SKIN & LEOPARD
OCTOPUS' GARDEN 1-4
THE OWLERY X 2
ZEBRA STRIPES AND ZEBRA
JELLYFISH BEANIE HAT
SNAGON 1 and 2
SNEAGLE 1 and 2
GIRAFFE PATCHES AND GIRAFFE
TURTLES 1 and 2
GORILLA LUNCH AND GORILLA
FLAME PLANTS & ROARING TIGER
BEWITCHED FOREST 1 and 2
JELLYFISH 1 and 2
ARACHNO-STACEANS X 2
BALLERINA & BEAR CLAWS
BULL RUN X 2
ELEPHANT FRONT & BUSH BUNNY
NATURE 1 X 2
NATURE 2 X 2
ELEPHANT CHARGE X 2
PEACOCK & MOON FOREST
ROYAL GARDENS X 2
DOGS X 2
FOLIAGE SPREAD X 2
ABOUT THE AUTHOR

THIS BOOK CONTAINS MANY HIDDEN CREATURES WHICH ARE SHOWN IN THE TREE OF LIFE IN THE FIRST FOUR PAGES. YOU WILL DISCOVER THESE CHARACTERS AS YOU COMPLETE EACH DESIGN. HOW MANY CAN YOU FIND OF THE FOLLOWING?

DIAMOND PIRANHA
HUMMING BIRD
ROYAL FROG
CURIOUS ROOK
FEATHERED PARROT
SCORPION
TREE LIZARD
DOUBLE TONGUED LIZARD
LADY BIRD
CENTREPEDE
DIAMOND SPIDER
BUTTTER-MOTH

ACKNOWLEDGMENTS:

I'D LIKE TO ACKNOWLEDGE YOU FOR PURCHASING THIS BOOK MAKING IT POSSIBLE FOR ME TO CREATE NEW WORLDS, PLACES, SCENES AND CREATURES. I'D LOVE TO CREATE MANY MORE WORLDS WITH YOUR HELP.

IMAGINATION, NATURE, TIME AND SPACE ARE WHAT MAKE IT ALL POSSIBLE

Tester Page

Tester Page

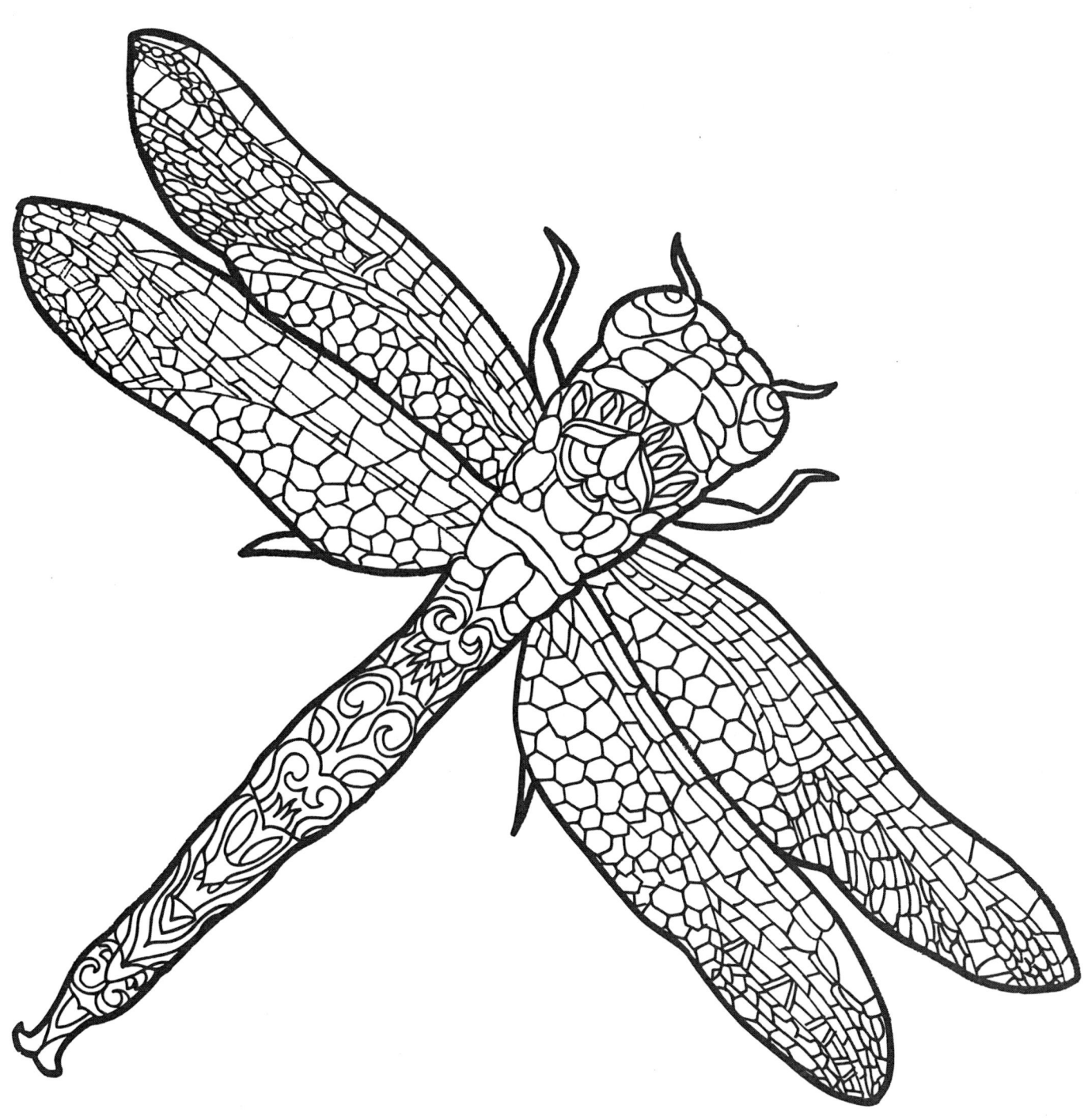

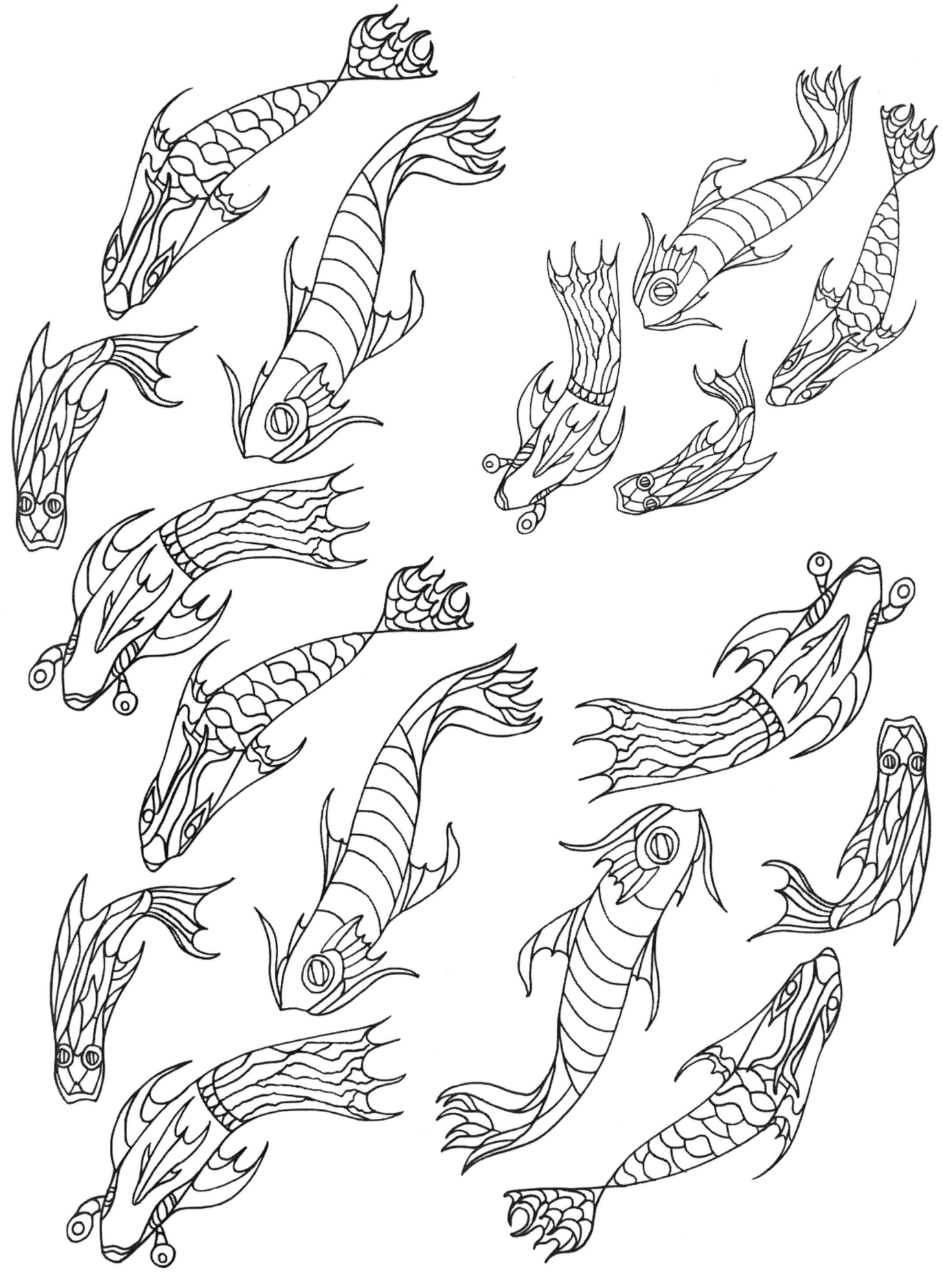

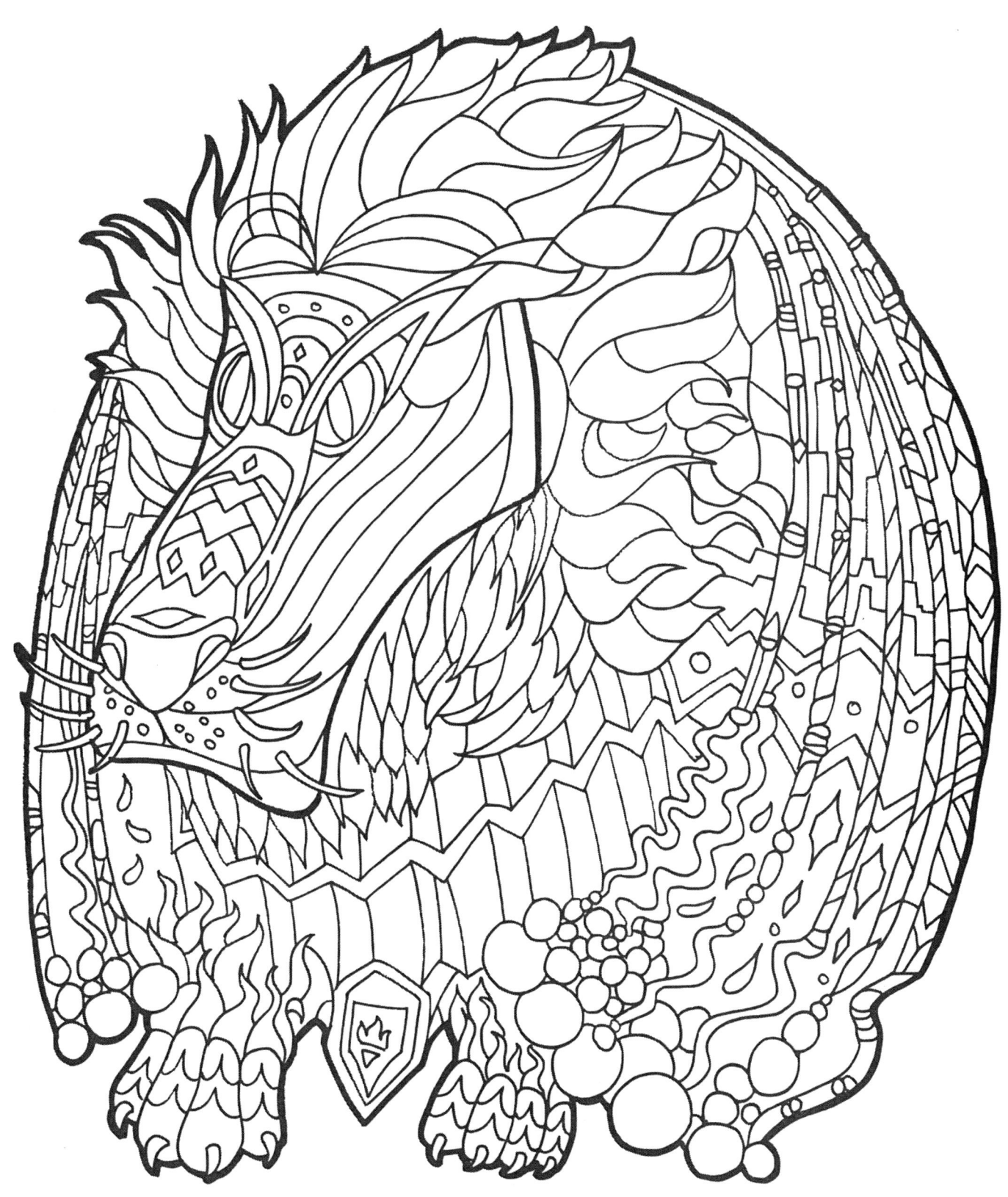

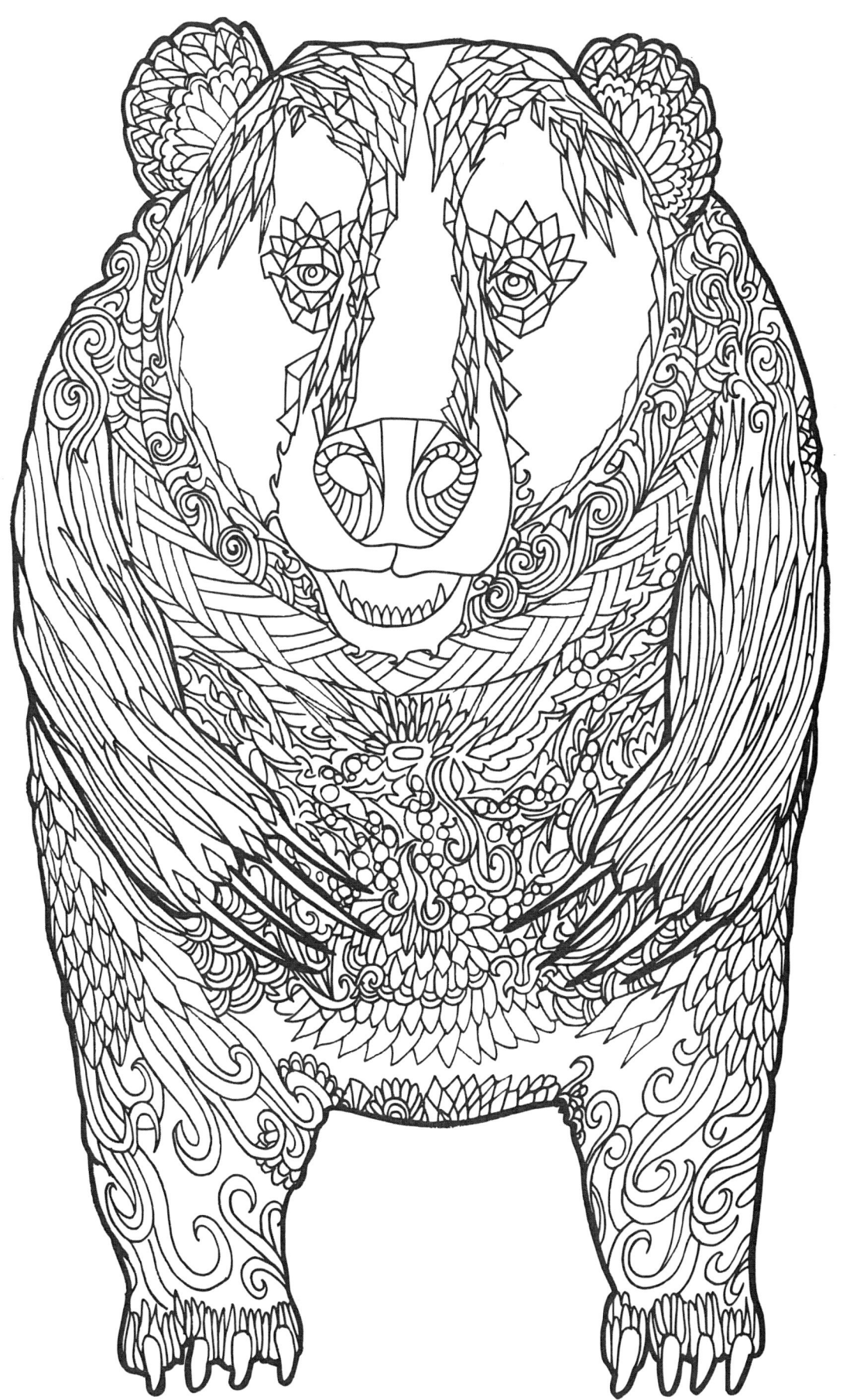

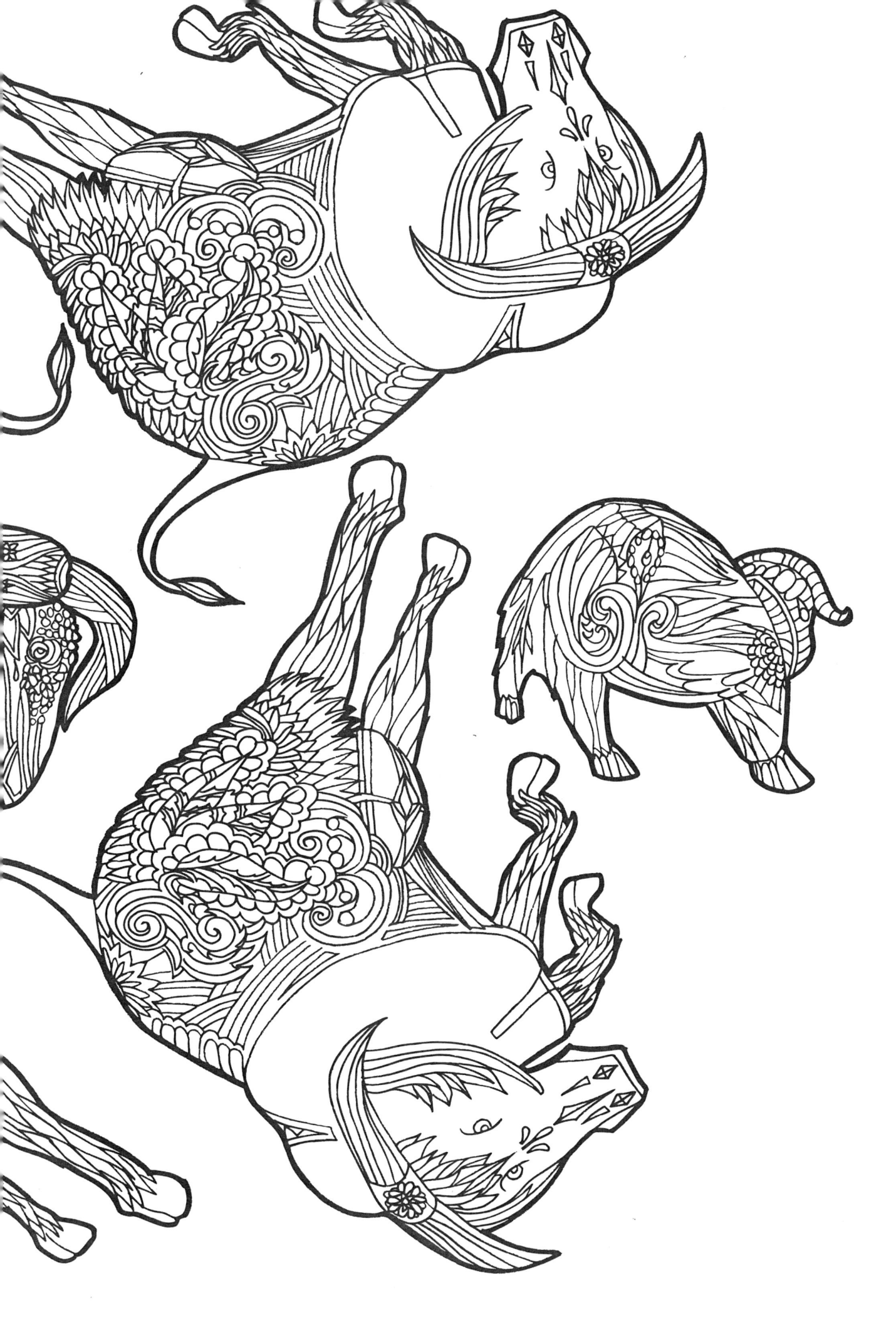

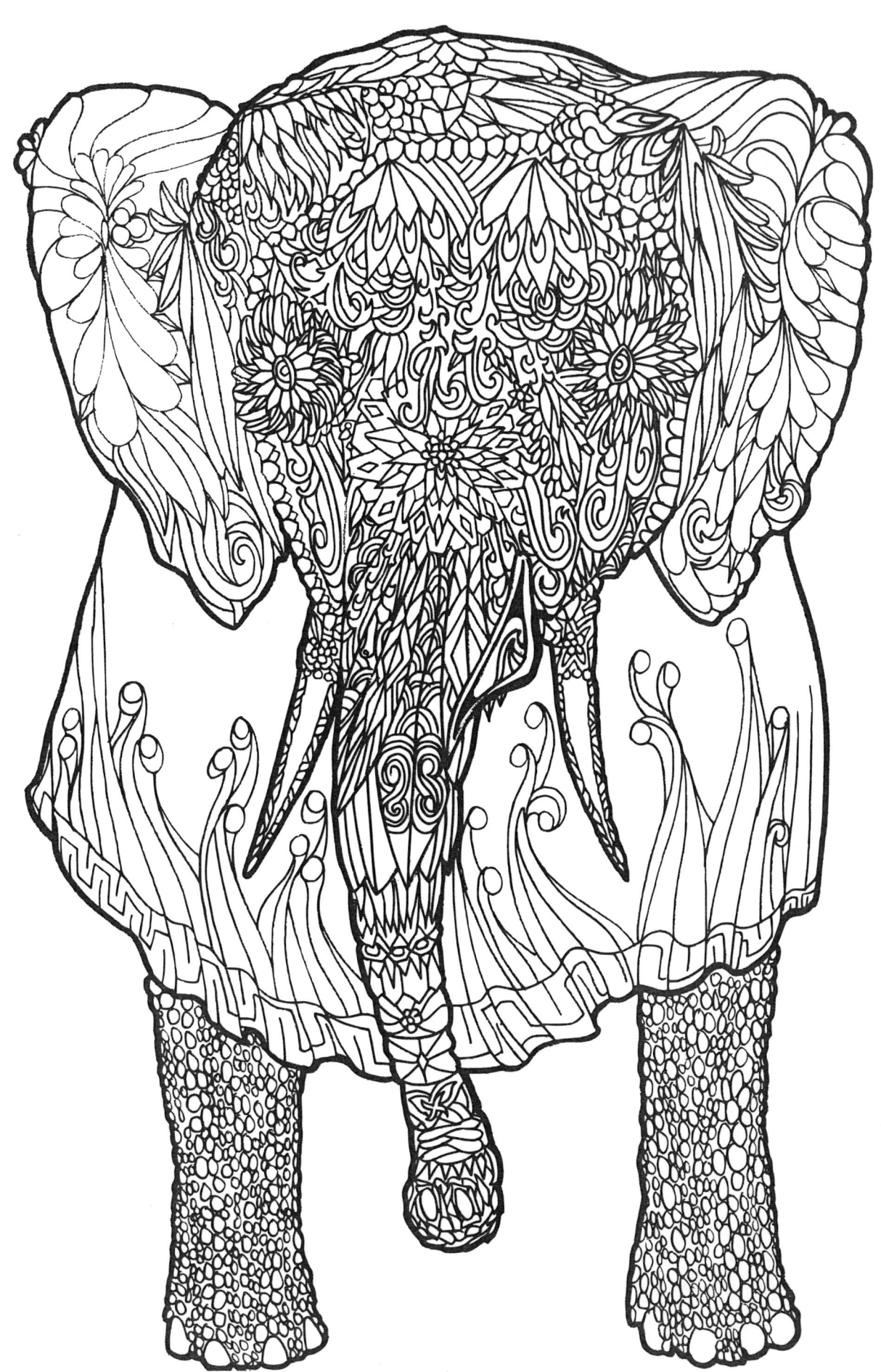

☆ ☆ ☆ ☆

CHALLENGE STAR RATING:

The level of difficulty for each illustration in this book has been given a challenge rating - see below

1 star = easiest
☆
2 stars = hard
☆ ☆
3 stars advanced
☆ ☆ ☆
4 stars expert
☆ ☆ ☆ ☆
5 stars = colouring ninja!
☆ ☆ ☆ ☆ ☆

☆ ☆ ☆ ☆

How many creatures from the image above are hidden throughout this enchanted colouring book?

☆ ☆ ☆ ☆

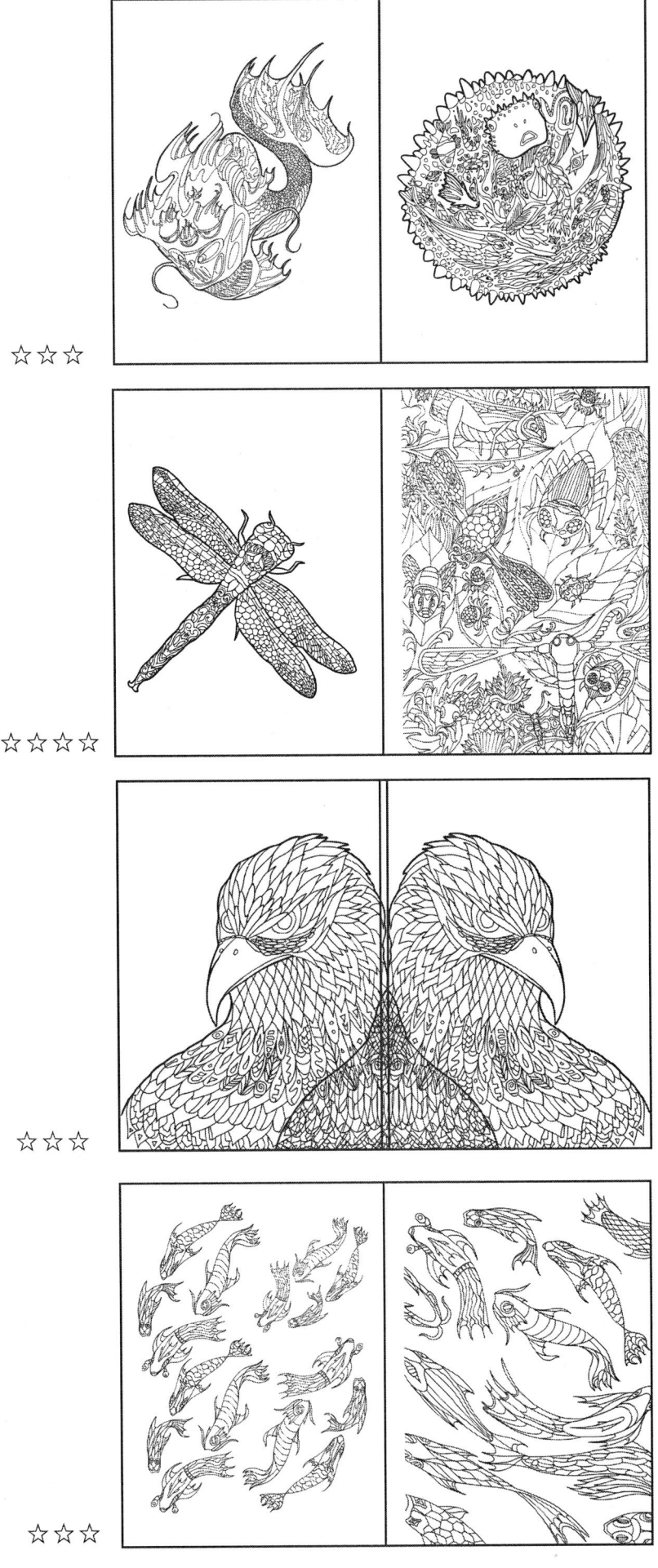

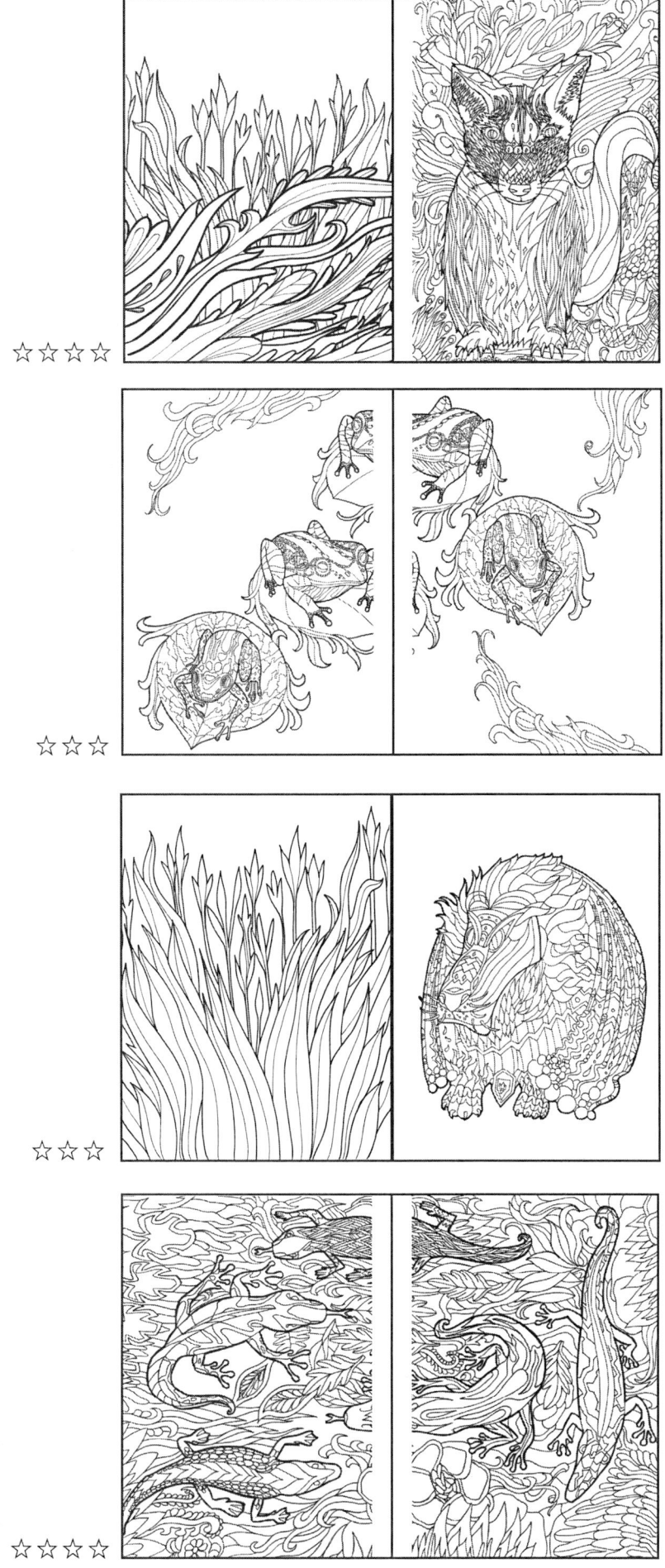

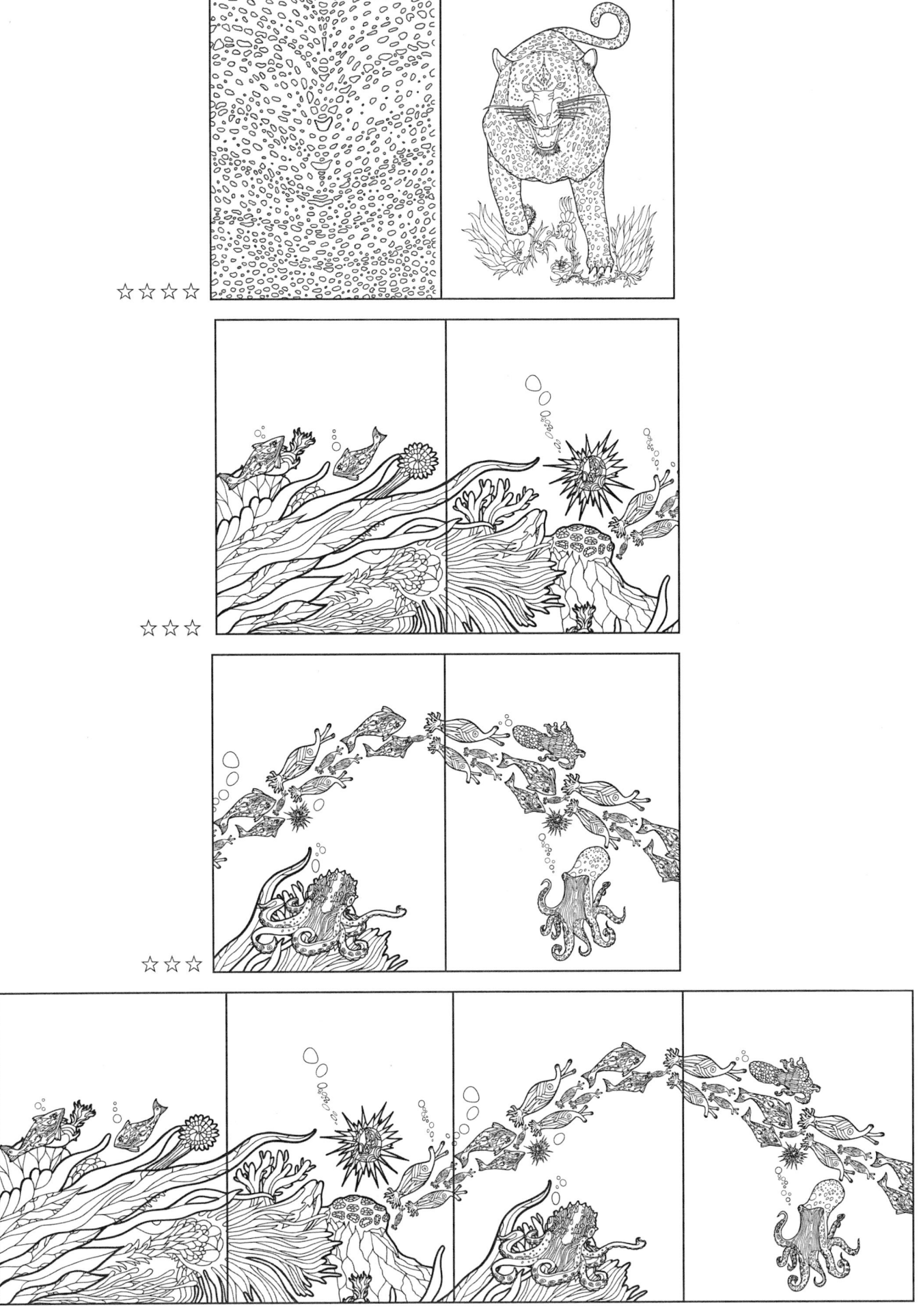

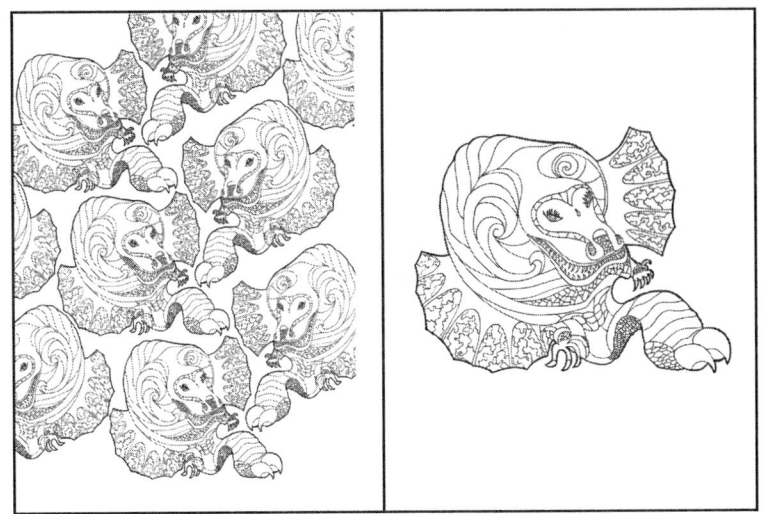

☆☆☆☆

☆☆☆

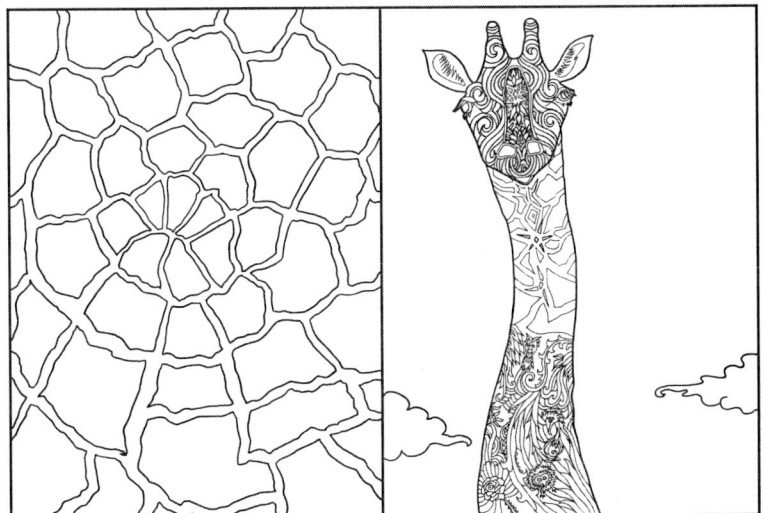

☆☆

☆☆☆☆

☆☆☆☆

☆☆☆☆

☆☆☆

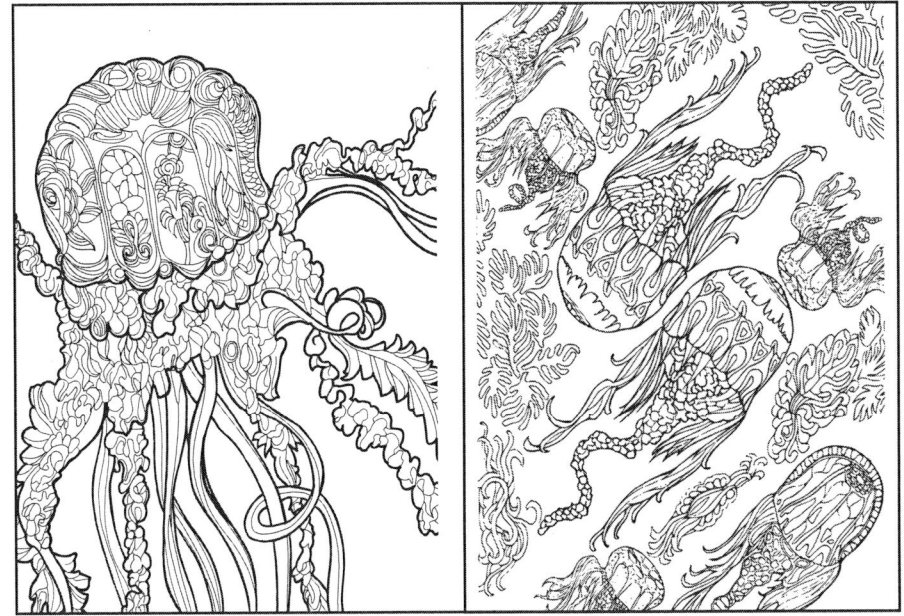

☆☆☆☆

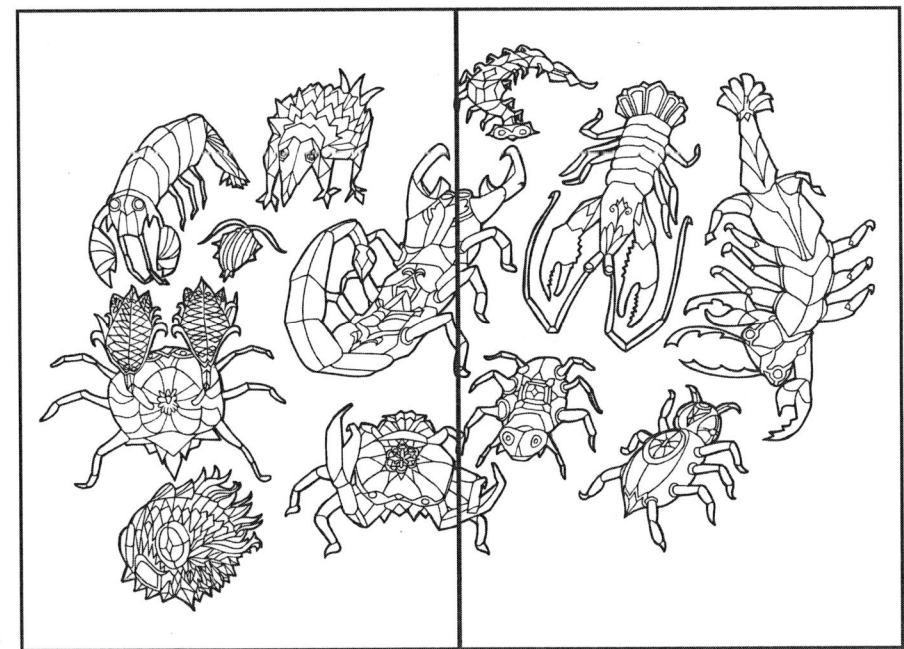

☆☆☆

☆☆☆

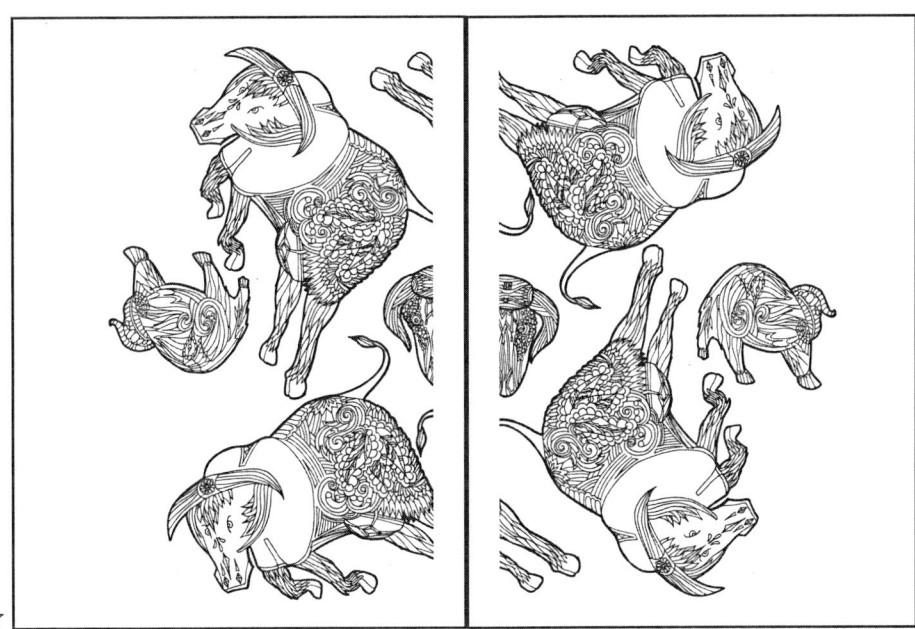

☆☆☆

☆☆☆☆☆

☆☆☆☆

☆☆☆

☆☆☆

☆☆☆☆☆

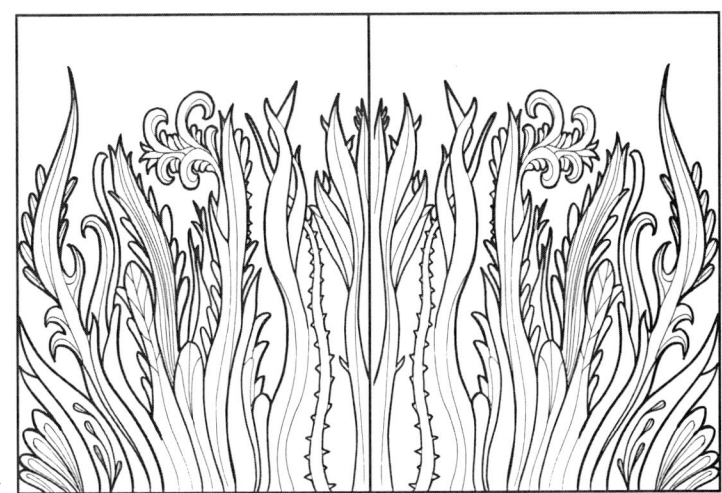
☆☆☆

☆☆☆

☆☆☆

THANK YOU

...if you enjoyed this title and are interested in pre-ordering future titles:
Dreams & Nightmares©
and A Walk In The City©
from the series:

CHROMA-THERAPY ©

Let me know. I am always happy to hear from readers/collaborators/
Publishers: cdkingbooks@gmail.com

ABOUT THE AUTHOR

Christopher D' King is a designer/engineer and an illustrator local to Oxfordshire. Having designed medical products, domestic appliances and automotive products for some of the biggest names out there, this is a refreshing departure from the machine-processed world which usually occupies his mind.

Using skills which were developed by tapping into the creative part of his brain, while out running and after being inspired by illustrations he had seen, he realized there was something familiar about the line-work and felt compelled to start drawing in this way and has not stopped since. The need to produce something physical and use the creation of this book as a method to channel and calm his own mind – this is the first in a series of inspired illustrations, which are not overly fussy about being symmetric, or perfect. He works in
pencil, and then traces this into pen and is developing and growing this technique and in confidence with each stroke.

The inspiration for a lot of the designs is born through a need to express something which is less ephemeral than pixels on an lcd screen. There's something deeply
satisfying about producing something which is ordered and describes something as random as nature in a few elegant lines.
www.cdkingbooks.com
@cdkingbooks